When God's People Pray

six sessions on the
transforming power of prayer

Jim Cymbala

with Stephen and Amanda Sorenson

bestselling author of **Fresh Wind, Fresh Fire**

ZONDERVAN®

ZONDERVAN.com/
AUTHORTRACKER
follow your favorite authors

ZONDERVAN®

When God's People Pray Participant's Guide
Copyright © 2007 by Jim Cymbala

Requests for information should be addressed to:

Zondervan, *Grand Rapids, Michigan 49530*

ISBN-10: 0-310-26734-X
ISBN-13: 978-0-310-26734-8

Published in association with the literary agency of Ann Spangler and Company, 1420 Pontiac Road S.E., Grand Rapids, MI 49506.

Interior design by Beth Shagene

Printed in the United States of America

08 09 10 11 12 • 20 19 18 17 16 15 14 13 12 11

Contents

Introduction

Our God loves us deeply and longs to be in a relationship in which we receive the spiritual and physical blessings he wants to give us. We, as individuals and as churches, suffer great loss when we fail to ask God for these blessings. These blessings can change our lives, invigorate our churches, transform our communities, and even alter the course of history! Best of all, they are available to every believer and every church if we will only pray for them in faith and obedience.

My desire through this video series is to help God's people discover prayer as our lifeline to him—our source of strength and abundant blessing. I want to help God's people engage in serious prayer and become a living display of what God—and he alone—can accomplish here on earth. I don't want any of us to suffer the tragedy of a life summed up by these words from Scripture: "You do not have, because you do not ask God" (James 4:2).

By God's grace, I pray that this video series will instruct, inspire, and assist God's people in discovering a new life of asking and receiving from God.

Jim Cymbala

Session One

God's Heart for Us

> *At that time people began to call on the name of the LORD.*
> GENESIS 4:26, TNIV

INTRODUCTION (6 MINUTES)

DVD Introduction by Jim Cymbala

Question to Think About

What do you think Christians and the churches they attend miss out on when calling on God in prayer is not an essential part of their life and worship?

DVD TEACHING SEGMENT (9 MINUTES)

Notes

God is rich in mercy to all who call on him

Prayer: the evidence of true faith

God answers prayer

Life's problems remind us to call on God

No place to go but God

GROUP EXPLORATION (18 MINUTES)

Discussion

1. What were your thoughts as Jim explained how people who really believe in God instinctively call on him in petition and praise?

> "The essence of all religion is people not only trusting God, but trusting him enough to call on his name in prayer so that they actually experience his gracious provision in their lives."
>
> **From the video**

2. To what degree do you think people in our culture (ourselves included) are aware of this instinct?

3. Jim says that God is a prayer-answering God who is rich in mercy to everyone who calls on him. When God responds to our prayers with mercy, what impact does it have on us, and what does it reveal to us about God?

4. As Christians, we believe that God already knows our needs, so what do you think might be his purpose in waiting for us to ask him to meet our needs before he takes action on our behalf?

Bible Discovery

1. What does Scripture say God will do when people turn to him in faith and wholeheartedly call on his name in prayer? (See Proverbs 15:29; Jeremiah 33:2–3; Matthew 7:7–8; Luke 18:7–8.)

"The Lord cherishes his people, and out of that love flows his desire to bless them. It is through these unmistakable blessings that others can witness God's goodness and declare, 'Look what the Lord has done!'"
Breakthrough Prayer,
p. 19

2. Scripture reveals valuable insight into God's character and commitment in relationship to his people.

   a. What is it about God that leads him to respond to those who cry out to him? (See Psalm 86:5–7; Psalm 89:8; Ephesians 2:4–5.)

   b. What response does God's faithfulness in answering prayer inspire in the hearts of his people? (See Deuteronomy 4:7; Psalm 4:3; Psalm 9:9–10.)

DVD PRAYER STORY (14 MINUTES)

> "The blessing of God is something very real and tangible. It can change a man's life, transform a neighborhood, invigorate a church, and even alter the course of history."
>
> *Breakthrough Prayer*, pp. 9–10

Group Discussion

1. When Wanda first prayed with Danny out loud, in public, what do you think began to happen in his life? Why do you think he continued to allow her to pray for him?

2. No matter how far away from God Danny ran, he could not forget Wanda's simple promise: "The day you call on the name of the Lord, he is going to set you free." Would you have expected such a simple, basic message to make such a great difference in Danny's life? Why or why not?

3. Why was it important for Wanda to have a whole team of people praying for Danny? What impact do you think seeing the fruit of their prayers in Danny's changed life had on those faithful believers?

WRAP-UP (13 MINUTES)

Closing DVD Comments from Jim Cymbala

Personal Reflection

God has chosen prayer as his channel of blessing and is waiting to answer us and supply our needs. He uses our everyday troubles to remind us that we need him to intervene in our lives and that we need to take prayer seriously and call on him passionately.

Think for several minutes about the difference the promise of 1 John 5:14–15 makes in your life: "This is the confidence we have in approaching God: that if we ask anything according to his will, he hears us. And if we know that he hears us—whatever we ask—we know that we have what we asked of him."

Now consider how you are approaching God as you face the challenges of your life:

- To what extent are you drawn to God, eagerly praying and anticipating his blessing?

- To what extent do you try to face challenges on your own, without God's help? What is the result?

- To what extent are you confident that God will keep his promises and meet your needs when you call on him?

Group Prayer

Briefly share a few needs and seemingly insurmountable problems you face. Then begin praying together. Praise God for who he is and what he has revealed to you during this session. Trust him enough to call on his name and ask him for help. Let today be the day you arise and talk to the Father from your hearts. Let this be the day you experience a breakthrough moment in which you receive help through the loving power of your prayer-answering God.

> "Does Almighty God really need our help? Of course not. But when the Lord's method for accomplishing his purpose includes you and me, then it is both a wonderful privilege and a sacred responsibility for us to respond with faith ... [and witness] the awesome power of a prayer-answering God."
>
> *Breakthrough Prayer*, p. 47

PERSONAL JOURNEY: TO DO ON YOUR OWN

God loves you deeply and longs to be in relationship with you. His blessings are tangible and life-changing, and he makes those blessings available to everyone who calls on him. You can bank on the promise of Philippians 4:6–7: "Do not be anxious about anything, but in everything, by prayer and petition, with thanksgiving, present your requests to God. And the peace of God, which transcends all understanding, will guard your hearts and your minds in Christ Jesus."

> "God is deeply concerned when his children are burdened by anxiety, in much the way parents are concerned about their children. It is tragic that we often worry ourselves to death when God's supernatural peace is only a prayer away."
>
> *Breakthrough Prayer*, p. 153

Bible Discovery

The Bible is full of examples of God's people who have gone before you and held nothing back when they asked God for help. A few of these examples are listed in the following chart. As you read about the needs and experiences of these people, consider what an awesome privilege it is to come to God's throne of grace. Write down how God answered these needy people who called on him from their hearts' deepest desires. Then think about your need to call out to God for help: write it down and start praying.

Bible Passage	Need(s) Expressed	God's Response	My Need for ...
Exodus 15:22–27			Physical provision:
1 Samuel 1:1–11, 19–20, 27–28			Hope in personal suffering:
1 Kings 8:22–30; 9:1–3			God's presence:
1 Chronicles 4:10			God's blessing:

Bible Passage	Need(s) Expressed	God's Response	My Need for ...
Ezra 8:21–23, 31–32			Safety:
Psalm 5:1–3, 12; 34:4–10			Everyday help and deliverance:
Acts 12:5–17			Rescue from evil intent:

Starting today, call on God with your whole heart! Tell him your needs, desires, hopes, and dreams. Pour out your heart before him and invite him into your life situation.

My Personal Prayer Journal

Is any one of you in trouble? He should pray.
JAMES 5:13

Use the following pages to write down your prayer requests, praises, thoughts about God and prayer, and so on. You might, for example, thank God in writing for the opportunity you have to call on his name, knowing that he is listening and will act in love on your behalf. You might jot down specific requests and what you would like to see God do in a particular situation. You might list some things that cause you to drift away from the practice of prayer and the things that draw you toward God in prayer. When fears, needs, and unmet desires surface in the days and weeks ahead, and you need God's help to stay on track, write them down.

Most important, get in the habit of prayer. Continue to pray, calling on the name of the Lord regularly. May this record of your prayer journey be a reminder of where you have been and an encouragement for what God will do as you continue to call on his name!

My Personal Prayer Journal

_If any of you lacks wisdom, you should ask God, who gives gener-
ously to all without finding fault, and it will be given to you._
JAMES 1:5, TNIV

The Amazing Power of Prayer

> *In the same way, the Spirit helps us in our weakness.*
> *We do not know what we ought to pray for, but the Spirit himself*
> *intercedes for us with groans that words cannot express.*
> ROMANS 8:26

INTRODUCTION (5 MINUTES)

DVD Introduction by Jim Cymbala

Question to Think About

Who are the people you would describe as men and women of prayer, and what evidence of the Holy Spirit's equipping and empowerment have you seen in their lives? In what ways have you seen God use them to accomplish his work?

DVD TEACHING SEGMENT (12 MINUTES)

Notes

Prayer—made possible by the Holy Spirit

God's work—accomplished as God pours out his Spirit

The need for ministry in prayer

A battle to proclaim God's house as a house of prayer

"Lord, teach us to pray"

GROUP EXPLORATION (18 MINUTES)

Discussion

1. Jim pointed out that the disciples asked Jesus to teach them how to pray—not how to preach! What do you think is significant about their request?

> "There's no telling what God can do when God's people begin to pray."
>
> From the video

How might the life and ministry of our churches change if we shared the disciples' attitude and desire for prayer?

2. Why do we need a fresh outpouring of the Holy Spirit to not only accomplish God's work, but to pray for that work and how God wants us to participate in it?

What happens when we lack the empowerment of the Spirit and try to depend on our own abilities and intellect?

3. Jim says that prayer "isn't a neat little thing you control." In fact, he presents it, in part, as work, travail, staying up all hours of the night in spiritual battle. How do these images compare with your understanding of the nature of prayer?

4. As you consider the biblical truths and experiences Jim shared in the video, what excites you about prayer?

What are your concerns or fears about prayer?

Bible Discovery

1. When the disciples said to Jesus, "Lord, teach us to pray," they knew that the secret to his strength and power was rooted in his communion with his heavenly Father. So let's look at a few moments of Jesus' life that the disciples surely witnessed so we can see what they saw and catch a glimpse of how much Jesus recognized and depended on the power of prayer as he lived on earth.

> "No matter the society or culture, the city or town, God has never lacked the power to work through available people to glorify his name."
>
> *Fresh Wind, Fresh Fire,* p. 97

Scripture Passage	How and Where Jesus Prayed	God's Powerful Work Accomplished
Mark 1:21, 35–39		
Luke 3:21–22; 4:1–2, 13		
Luke 5:15–16		
Luke 6:12–16		

2. According to Zechariah 4:6, what is our true source of power
   for accomplishing God's work?

3. Jim shared a powerful example of the Holy Spirit's leading
   when he revealed details of his preparation for preaching in
   Indianapolis. Such examples are not unusual when God's
   people rely on the Holy Spirit's empowerment to accomplish
   his work. Read Acts 16:6–10 to see an example of the power
   and leading of the Holy Spirit in the apostle Paul's life.

   a. What happened when Paul and his companions tried to
      enter the province of Asia to spread the gospel?

   b. In what way did God eventually reveal his will to Paul?
      How did Paul respond?

c. In what ways has the Holy Spirit revealed God's will to you?
   What impact did that leading have on you, how did you
   respond to it, and what was the result?

DVD PRAYER STORY (14 MINUTES)

> "To go into the power of
> the gospel, or of prayer,
> or the Holy Spirit, or
> divine love is to plunge
> ever deeper and deeper
> into God's well. Every
> man or woman used by
> God has gone **down**
> into this vast reservoir."
>
> *Fresh Wind, Fresh Fire,*
> p. 117

Group Discussion

1. When Sylvia Glover's friend began praying for her, do you think she had any idea what a prayer warrior Sylvia would become? Even though Sylvia considered herself to be a "lost cause," what do you think motivated her friend not only to pray, but to fast and pray, for Sylvia's salvation?

2. At first, the great needs in her life drove Sylvia to pray, but today Sylvia prays for an additional reason. What has she seen and experienced that drives her to pray?

3. Sylvia shared about how important it has been for her to "turn off" all distractions and focus intently on time with God in prayer. What are some of the distractions we need to deal with in order to focus on prayer, and what role does fasting play in our ability to pray?

WRAP-UP (11 MINUTES)

Closing DVD Comments from Jim Cymbala

Personal Reflection

This session has focused on the powerful role of the Holy Spirit in prayer. We have witnessed examples of the power of prayer in the lives of people and the church, and we have caught a glimpse of the power of the Spirit in guiding us in prayer and in answering our prayers. Now it is time to begin experiencing that power in our lives.

God longs for each of us to draw close to him in prayer. Ephesians 6:18 implores us to "pray in the Spirit on all occasions with all kinds of prayers and requests."

- Do you long for God deeply enough to approach his throne of grace with all of your prayers and requests?

- Are you willing to begin asking the Holy Spirit to pour himself into your life?

- Are you eager for the Spirit to manifest himself to you in new, fresh, and more powerful ways?

Then plunge forward into the adventure of prayer! The Spirit is waiting to teach, lead, and empower you to accomplish the mighty, miraculous works of God!

Group Prayer

Before you begin to pray together, confess your sins and ask God to anoint you with his Spirit. Then take a few minutes to share a few of the things you believe God wants to accomplish through prayer.

As you pray, praise God for allowing you to enter his presence in prayer and for listening to you every time you pray. Pray for revival. Pray for a fresh work of the Holy Spirit in your lives—in the life of your family, your small group, your church, your community, your country. Ask God to fill and empower you with a fresh supply of the Holy Spirit to carry out his work.

> "As we take time to call on the Lord, confess our sins, clear the decks of anything that would hinder an answer from God, we're going to see miraculous things happen."
>
> **From the video**

PERSONAL JOURNEY: TO DO ON YOUR OWN

It's no secret that God wants you to pray. After all, prayer is essential to everything God wants his people and his church to accomplish. For that reason he has sent the Holy Spirit to equip and empower you to be an effective person of prayer. He longs to teach you to pray and accomplish great things in and through you. So keep asking God to pour out his Spirit upon you. Ask him daily for a fresh supply of the Holy Spirit and keep learning as he teaches you to pray.

> "When it comes to being led by the Lord, there are no simple formulas that apply to every situation. We need to learn to follow God's leading day by day."
>
> **Breakthrough Prayer, p. 205**

Bible Discovery

God's Word, the Bible, is filled with commands to pray. The verses below and on the next page include just a few of those commands. Look up each one and write out the prayer command(s). As you commit yourself to the practice of daily prayer, reread these commands. They will help teach you and encourage you to keep on praying.

• 1 Chronicles 16:11

• Isaiah 55:6

• Matthew 26:41

• Romans 12:12

• Ephesians 6:18

• Colossians 4:2

• 1 Thessalonians 5:17

My Personal Prayer Journal

Let us then approach the throne of grace with confidence, so that
we may receive mercy and find grace to help us in our time of need.
HEBREWS 4:16

Use the following pages to write down your prayer requests, praises, thoughts about God and prayer, and so on. You might, for example, write down some of your praises for answers to prayer. You might write down some of the wonderful things that will happen as God pours out his Spirit in response to your prayers.

Most important, continue to pray, calling on the name of the Lord regularly. May this record of your prayer journey be a testimony to the power of prayer and the dynamic, empowering work of the Holy Spirit. May it encourage you to approach God's throne of grace with confidence.

My Personal Prayer Journal

_The prayer of a righteous person is powerful and effective.
Elijah was a human being, even as we are. He prayed earnestly
that it would not rain, and it did not rain on the land for three
and a half years. Again he prayed, and the heavens gave rain,
and the earth produced its crops._

JAMES 5:16–18, TNIV

Session Three
Obedience in Prayer

If I had cherished sin in my heart, the Lord would not have listened;
but God has surely listened and heard my voice in prayer.
PSALM 66:18–19

INTRODUCTION (5 MINUTES)

DVD Introduction by Jim Cymbala

Question to Think About

What is your understanding of the connection between our prayers, our obedience to God and his Word, and the way in which God responds to our prayers?

DVD TEACHING SEGMENT #1 (7 MINUTES)

Notes

Fighting the attacks of the enemy

The truth about underhanded dealings with God

Walking in the light

GROUP EXPLORATION #1 (12 MINUTES)

Discussion

1. Jim speaks about prayer in terms of it being a battleground where Satan consistently targets his attacks against Christians. What do you think Satan is trying to accomplish by this strategy, and how effective is it?

> "If we really want to pray with power, we need to break through into greater holiness. We don't need a formula or a method for praying. But we do need to live with purity and simplicity rather than with carnality, hype, and hardness."
>
> *Breakthrough Prayer,*
> pp. 173–174

2. Why does God refuse to hear us and bless us when we choose to keep practicing sin rather than obeying his Word?

What is the problem when we think we can hide our sin and "fool" God into blessing us anyway?

3. As we grow in prayer and seek the blessings God has for us, why is it so important that we confess our sins to God and keep asking him to reveal any unconfessed sins in our lives?

What is easy about confessing our sin on a regular basis?

What about it is difficult?

Bible Discovery

1. It is easy for us to minimize the seriousness of our sin. We can easily convince ourselves that our sin doesn't really matter if no one knows about it or if it doesn't really hurt anyone. If we can keep our sin hidden from view, we tend to think we're home free. God, however, has a different view. In the following Scripture passages, note how seriously God views the sin of his people and how strongly he warns of the consequences of ongoing disobedience, particularly in reference to prayer.

> "Because Satan understands the potential of prayer far better than we, he has developed cunning strategies to clog the asking-receiving channel. An unforgiving spirit, bitterness, secret sexual sins — the list is endless — can stymie our praying. Every sin we hide and justify becomes a hindrance to bold, confident prayer to the Father."
>
> *Breakthrough Prayer*, p. 86

   a. In the vision he gave to Ezekiel, how did God promise he would respond to the idolatrous people of Judah? (See Ezekiel 8:17–18; 20:31.)

b. According to the prophet Isaiah, how did God say he would respond to the prayers of his people if they continued to disobey him? (See Isaiah 1:15; 59:1–2.)

2. Given the gravity of our sin in God's eyes, we can be grateful that God is as abundant in mercy as he is serious about sin. How does he respond when, with sincere, repentant hearts, we request his mercy? (See 2 Chronicles 7:14; 1 John 1:9.)

3. According to 1 John 3:21–22, what is absolutely necessary for empowered prayer?

DVD PRAYER STORY (12 MINUTES)

> "To lose [God's] blessing
> because we prefer
> to cling to our sins is to
> suffer the most profound
> tragedy imaginable."
> *Breakthrough Prayer,*
> *p. 26*

Group Discussion

1. What happens to our relationship with God and other people when we, like Craig, harbor bitterness or other sins? What evidence did you see that Craig's bitterness against his father affected his relationship with God?

2. What blessings began to flow as Craig opened up before God
   in prayer, confessed his anger, and dealt with his bitterness?
   How deeply and for how long had Craig needed that blessing?

3. Why do you think it is so easy for us to discount our need
   to confess our sins and keep trying to survive on our own
   instead of bringing our sins to God and asking for his
   forgiveness and healing?

DVD TEACHING SEGMENT #2 (6 MINUTES)

Notes

The privileges of walking in the light

Unexpected preparation for a critical moment

Drawn aside for special times of prayer

GROUP EXPLORATION #2 (6 MINUTES)

Discussion

1. In what ways is preparatory prayer distinct from our daily prayer life, and in what ways is it connected with our daily prayer life?

> "The Lord is faithful. As we walk obediently in the light even as he is in the light, he has a wonderful ability to not only answer prayer but to draw us aside for special times of preparatory prayer."
>
> **From the video**

What is the purpose of preparatory prayer, and why is it so important to spend time in this type of prayer when God directs us to do so?

2. Like the disciples in the Garden of Gethsemane, we have no clue when critical moments in our lives are about to happen. Discuss some of the ways you anticipate that preparatory prayer could help you face critical moments in your life.

   What could be at risk if you miss out on the times of preparatory prayer God makes available to you?

3. Jim said, "As we stay open to the Lord and feel those wooings and drawings to spend time with him, let's obey them." How does God communicate these "wooings and drawings" to us?

How do we cultivate our sensitivity to them and learn to distinguish them from our own thoughts and desires?

WRAP-UP (12 MINUTES)

Closing DVD Comments from Jim Cymbala

Personal Reflection

In order to have an open prayer channel with God—one that enables us to talk freely and sincerely with him and allows his response to flow down to us unhindered—we must walk "in the light" as described in 1 John 1:5–7:

> *God is light; in him there is no darkness at all.*
> *If we claim to have fellowship with him yet walk in the darkness,*
> *we lie and do not live by the truth. But if we walk in the light,*
> *as he is in the light, we have fellowship with one another,*
> *and the blood of Jesus, his Son, purifies us from all sin.*

Walking in the light means we cannot cling to disobedience, unconfessed sin, hypocrisy, or any other "deeds of darkness" (Romans 13:12). We cannot live in disobedience and live in God's blessing at the same time. So take several minutes to be alone with God right now. Open your heart to him and clear away any darkness that is hindering your communication and blocking the pure, healing power of his response.

- Ask God to convict you of your sin.
- Ask God to shine his light into any dark areas of your life.
- Ask God to show you anything that is hindering your communion with him.

Group Prayer

> "If we want to see answers from God, we can't be dealing in an underhanded way with our Creator. We can't practice sin and ask God, who is holy, to help us in another area while we are holding onto the sin that his Word tells us he is totally against and opposed to."
>
> From the video

Together, begin by praying out loud the first two verses of Psalm 32 (TNIV):

> *Blessed are those*
> *whose transgressions are forgiven,*
> *whose sins are covered.*
> *Blessed are those*
> *whose sin the LORD does not count against them*
> *and in whose spirit is no deceit.*

Then continue praying not only for your needs and problems, but that God would prepare and arm you for what he wants to accomplish through you.

PERSONAL JOURNEY: TO DO ON YOUR OWN

When our holy God issues his commands and personal orders for our lives, he always is motivated by love and wants to keep us in the center of his will and under the fountain of his countless blessings. That is why the psalmist writes, "The eyes of the LORD are on the righteous and his ears are attentive to their cry" (Psalm 34:15). Yet God's blessing is reserved for those who desire righteousness, for those who long with all their soul to walk in God's light and holiness.

> "Repentance is the only true 'deliverance' for Christians who find themselves in the grip of sin. It is the one sure road leading out of darkness into God's sunlight.... We need to repent and pray, remembering that the God who delights to show mercy is near, waiting for us to call on his name."
>
> *Breakthrough Prayer,*
> *pp. 53, 54*

Bible Discovery

Although walking a life of obedience through faith is something we may find difficult to do, it is essential for opening a channel for God's blessing. The Scripture passages on the next page clearly outline God's expectations—who he will hear and bless and who he will not hear. Read each passage and write out a profile of who God will listen to and who he will not. Refer to it often as you deepen your prayer life and walk with God.

Scripture Passage	Who God Hears	Who God Will Not Hear
1 Samuel 12:1, 14–15		
Psalm 37:4, 16–19		
Proverbs 15:8, 29		
John 9:30–31		
James 4:3		
1 Peter 3:12		
1 John 5:14–15		

In the life of a believer, repentance is not a one-time event, but an ongoing part of a walk with God. Godly people won't tolerate hidden sin in their lives and are quick to confess their disobedience and seek mercy from the Lord. So if you don't already do so, diligently pray during the coming days for God's conviction of sin. Ask God to teach you how to be completely honest with him and stop holding on to sin — including "secret" sins. Confess your sins before him, asking for his forgiveness. Ask him to purge you of all that is unrighteous and to give you a personal revival that will bear fruit to the praise of the glory of his name.

My Personal Prayer Journal

*For the eyes of the Lord are on the righteous
and his ears are attentive to their prayer,
but the face of the Lord is against those who do evil.*
1 PETER 3:12

During this session, you have seen how sin affects your relationship with God and why it's important to confess your sins to him continually. Use the following pages not only to write down prayer requests, praises, and thoughts about God and prayer, but to journal about how your past or current sins have affected your relationship with God and hindered your prayer life. Pray honestly about these things and ask God to convict you of sin and expose any problem areas that continue to hinder you in prayer.

Remember, God longs to have an open channel with you so his answers to your prayers can come down unhindered! Continue to pray, confess your shortcomings, and grow in confidence as you call on the name of the Lord.

My Personal Prayer Journal

We know that God does not listen to sinners.
He listens to the godly person who does his will.
JOHN 9:31, TNIV

Session Four

The Word of God and Prayer

> *Faith comes from hearing the message,*
> *and the message is heard through the word of Christ.*
>
> ROMANS 10:17

INTRODUCTION (4 MINUTES)

DVD Introduction by Jim Cymbala

Question to Think About

How well do you know God's Word, and how does your knowledge of the Word affect your prayer life?

DVD TEACHING SEGMENT (8 MINUTES)

Notes

Praying the prayer of faith

Prayer and the Word

Holding on to God's promises

Enduring in prayer

GROUP EXPLORATION (18 MINUTES)

Discussion

1. Jim spoke about the difference between merely reciting our petitions to God and praying with faith and confidence that God will answer according to all he has promised. How would you describe the

> "Prayer is not overcoming God's reluctance. It is laying hold of God's willingness."
>
> George Mueller, 19th-century saint, quoted in *Breakthrough Prayer*, p. 83

differences in our attitude, faithfulness, and expectations when we pray in one way versus the other?

2. Why is reading the Bible and knowing what it says so vital to a meaningful, effective prayer life?

How would you describe what God's Word provides and accomplishes in relationship to prayer?

3. What do you find to be the most challenging aspect of enduring prayer—of continuing to pray faithfully and earnestly when the circumstances about which you are praying seem to go from bad to worse?

How do your prayers change when this happens?

What enables you to persevere?

4. Jim says that God never fails anyone who trusts him, yet in the midst of the ups and downs of life many of us are at least tempted to doubt this biblical truth. What happens to our faith and our prayer life when our trust in God falters?

What happens when we hold on and continue to trust God?

Bible Discovery

> "You must always relate the Word of God to prayer because it's the Word of God that produces faith that makes prayer vital and dynamic."
>
> **From the video**

1. God's Word and prayer go hand in hand. So in order to become people of prayer, we need to develop a vital relationship with the Word of God. We need to grow in the faith that comes from knowing the Bible and calling on God to fulfill his promises.

   a. We need to discover the power of God's Word. Note the words God uses to describe the power of his Word in Jeremiah 23:29 and Hebrews 4:12. To what extent do these words of living power describe your prayer life?

   b. What does God's Word—described in Psalm 19:7–8 as "law," "statutes," "precepts," and "commands"—accomplish? To what extent do we need the results of God's Word in our prayer life?

c. What, according to Deuteronomy 8:3 and Romans 15:4, does God's Word provide for us? To what extent do each of us need these things in our prayer life?

2. Many of the Psalms give us images of what a dynamic, honest, and powerful prayer life looks like. How do we know that the psalmist took God's Word seriously in the prayers of Psalm 1:1 – 3; 119:147 – 148?

DVD PRAYER STORY (14 MINUTES)

> "Miracles ... are going to continue to happen as people learn to read the Word of God, call upon the name of the Lord, and then see God answer their prayers."
>
> **From the video**

Group Discussion

1. When Roberta experienced what she calls her "dark night of the soul," what impact did the Word of God have on her heart, life, and experience of God's presence?

2. Roberta describes a time in her life when she "literally
   couldn't go anywhere without [her] Bible." Have you ever
   experienced a time when your hunger for God's Word was
   so great you couldn't live without it? If so, describe. If not,
   in what ways do you think your life would change if you were
   receiving that much life, health, and vitality from the Word
   of God every day?

3. What do you think it was like for Roberta to read, then
   experience the promise of Isaiah 58:6–9? How does her
   testimony of learning to rely on the life-giving promises of
   God encourage you and give you hope?

WRAP-UP (12 MINUTES)

Closing DVD Comments from Jim Cymbala

Personal Reflection

Because God understands how hard it is for us to realize that no situation is too big for him, he has filled the sacred Scriptures with reminders of his awesome power and promises of his faithfulness. We need these reminders as encouragement whenever we face those big, immovable "mountains" that challenge our faith.

A few of the many promises from God's Word are listed on pages 68–69. Read through those promises and take a few minutes to consider how they relate to your prayer relationship with God.

- In what ways do these promises encourage you to seek God in prayer?

- Which promises give you hope?

- In what ways have you seen God fulfill these promises in your life or the life of someone you know?

- For what things have you earnestly prayed for God's help?

- Which promises speak to that need?

- How would praying applicable promises back to God affect your prayer relationship with him?

- Which promise(s) speak to your area of greatest need right now?

Thank God for his faithfulness in keeping his promises. As you come together with your group to pray, begin praying back to God the promises that address your present needs.

Group Prayer

> "Why should any of us wait one more minute to receive what we need from God? . . . Let this be our day to experience a breakthrough moment in which we will receive help through the loving power of our prayer-answering God."
>
> *Breakthrough Prayer*, p. 158

As you pray together, ask the Holy Spirit to pour himself into your lives, to manifest himself in new, fresh, and more powerful ways. Thank God for his faithfulness in hearing the prayers of his obedient people and for fulfilling the promises found in his Word. Then begin praying back those promises to the God who delights in answering the prayers of his people.

Scripture Promises

"For I know the plans I have for you," declares the Lord,
"plans to prosper you and not to harm you,
plans to give you hope and a future.
Then you will call upon me and come and pray to me,
and I will listen to you."
JEREMIAH 29:11–12

God is our refuge and strength,
an ever-present help in trouble.
PSALM 46:1

"Though the mountains be shaken and the hills be removed,
yet my unfailing love for you will not be shaken
nor my covenant of peace be removed," says the Lord,
who has compassion on you.
ISAIAH 54:10

For God so loved the world,
that he gave his one and only Son,
that whoever believes in him
shall not perish but have eternal life.
JOHN 3:16

Ask and it will be given to you; seek and you will find;
knock and the door will be opened to you.
For everyone who asks receives; he who seeks finds;
and to him who knocks, the door will be opened.
MATTHEW 7:7–8

Cast your cares on the Lord *and he will sustain you;*
he will never let the righteous fall.
PSALM 55:22

The Lord *is close to the brokenhearted*
and saves those who are crushed in spirit.
PSALM 34:18

When the Chief Shepherd appears,
you will receive the crown of glory that will never fade away.
1 PETER 5:4

But the Lord is faithful, and he will strengthen
and protect you from the evil one.
2 THESSALONIANS 3:3

He will cover you with his feathers,
and under his wings you will find refuge;
his faithfulness will be your shield and rampart.
PSALM 91:4

If we confess our sins, he is faithful and just
and will forgive us our sins and purify us
from all unrighteousness.
1 JOHN 1:9

For the LORD God is a sun and shield:
the LORD bestows favor and honor;
no good thing does he withhold
from those whose walk is blameless.
PSALM 84:11

Blessed are the pure in heart,
for they will see God.
MATTHEW 5:8

If any of you lacks wisdom, he should ask God,
who gives generously to all without finding fault,
and it will be given to him.
JAMES 1:5

For God did not give us a spirit of timidity,
but a spirit of power, of love and of self-discipline.
2 TIMOTHY 1:7

PERSONAL JOURNEY: TO DO ON YOUR OWN

At various times during this session, Jim mentioned the importance of praying the prayer of faith. Faith is paramount in the Christian's daily life. Romans 1:17 states that "the righteous will live by faith," and Hebrews 11:6 says that "without faith it is impossible to please God." So it should not surprise us when the enemy seeks to breach our spiritual immune system by attacking our faith.

> "The great challenge is to keep praying and enduring in prayer and persevering in prayer until that moment of favor comes, when God does what he has promised to do."
>
> **From the video**

But God never fails those who trust in him, and he desires that we have the faith we need to approach his throne of grace. He wants us to be confident that he — our trustworthy, faithful God — will answer us. He wants us to experience dynamic, powerful prayer and rejoice in his answers. And he has given us his Word as a powerful weapon to help build up our faith in prayer and stand strong against the attacks of the enemy. No matter what has happened to us, no matter what our present circumstances may be, we can build our faith on the trustworthy character of God.

Bible Discovery

Read each of the Scripture passages on pages 71–72 and write down how you can know that God is trustworthy and will fulfill his promises. Write down specific things for which you will trust God based on these passages. Pray these passages and work on memorizing them so that God's faithfulness is ever before you. Ask God to pour out a fresh supply of his Spirit upon you and to make his promises ever more real to you.

- Deuteronomy 7:9

- Psalm 32:10

- Psalm 33:1 – 4

- Psalm 34:22

- Psalm 145:13

• Proverbs 30:5

It is a challenge to believe that no situation, however evil or entrenched, is beyond the scope of prayer. In theory we know that God can do anything, but often it is not easy to trust him when it comes time to pray (and to continue to pray) for specific people or situations. It's all the more difficult when things seem to get worse or when people ridicule you while you wait on God.

During such times you may be tempted to doubt the Word of God, but keep trusting God and praying. Cling to the Word and the faithfulness of God despite the negative circumstances you see around you. Select a prayer promise or a portion of Scripture that declares the faithfulness and trustworthiness of God and continue to pray his Word back to him until his answer comes. Ask and expect the Holy Spirit to guide and encourage you, to purge you of self-dependence so that you can keep trusting God with your most difficult challenges.

My Personal Prayer Journal

> *The statutes you have laid down are righteous;*
> *they are fully trustworthy.... Your promises have been*
> *thoroughly tested, and your servant loves them.*
> PSALM 119:138, 140

Continue to persevere in prayer, calling on God with the confidence that no situation is beyond his care and power. Establish your faith on God's unalterable Word even when your circumstances don't seem to improve. Use the following pages to write down what you experience as you seek to place your faith solely in God and trust him to answer you according to his promises.

My Personal Prayer Journal

Those who hope in me will not be disappointed.
ISAIAH 49:23

Why Prayer Matters

> *I urge, then, first of all, that requests, prayers,*
> *intercession and thanksgiving be made for everyone.*
> 1 TIMOTHY 2:1

INTRODUCTION (5 MINUTES)

DVD Introduction by Jim Cymbala

Question to Think About

Why is it so important—for us as well as for those for whom we pray—that we continue to intercede for people even when we don't feel like it or when their situations seem to get worse the more we pray?

DVD TEACHING SEGMENT #1 (7 MINUTES)

Notes

Intercessory prayer: a Christlike ministry

The heritage of intercessory prayer in the Scriptures

The power of intercessory prayer

DVD PRAYER STORY (13 MINUTES)

GROUP EXPLORATION #1 (15 MINUTES)

Discussion

1. To what extent have you considered intercessory prayer to be a vital ministry of the church?

> "God is so wonderful because he doesn't just bring you home. When he brings you home, he uses you to bring others. It's awesome!"
>
> **Vanessa Holland, from the video**

In what ways has what you have seen today expanded and inspired your view of the ministry of prayer?

2. As you consider Jim's teaching and Vanessa's story, why do you think intercessory prayer is so powerful and pleasing to God?

3. When believers commit to pray earnestly for other people, what can be the impact not only on those who are the recipients of their prayers but on those who pray, on the church, on others in the community?

Bible Discovery

The early Christians not only believed in the power of (and need for) intercessory prayer—they thrived on it. And when they prayed, God responded in amazing ways. Read the following passages and take note of the many needs for which the early Christians prayed.

> "Praying for another person is like touching God with one hand and touching the person with the other. That's what intercessory prayer is all about."
>
> **From the video**

Scripture Passage	Prayers of intercession for:
Acts 8:14–15	
Romans 15:31	
Ephesians 1:17–19	
Ephesians 3:16–19	
Ephesians 6:19–20	
2 Thessalonians 1:11	
Philemon 6	

- How important do you think intercession for these needs was in the life of the early church? How important is intercession for these (and similar) needs today?

- What has been your experience in praying for needs such as these?

- What do you think God will accomplish in your church if you take seriously the need for intercession in these areas? In what ways do you think your church will change as people exercise the privilege and responsibility of intercessory prayer?

DVD TEACHING SEGMENT #2 (6 MINUTES)

Notes

Never give up on prayer

Overwhelmed by the battle but never without hope

Nothing is impossible with God

GROUP EXPLORATION #2 (5 MINUTES)

> "God, who encourages and strengthens his people,
> often uses other believers to accomplish his purpose. . . .
> Not until heaven will we understand the greatness
> of those who prevailed in prayer for other believers."
>
> *Breakthrough Prayer*, pp. 183,188

Discussion

1. When we pray according to our moods, it's easy to give up
   on prayer when God's answers seem slow in coming. If we're
   committed to persevering, intercessory prayer, on what do we
   need to base our prayers so we can remain strong during the
   battle?

2. If you feel comfortable doing so, share things that have
   discouraged you in intercessory prayer.

What did you do to fight against Satan's discouragement?

What restored your faith and confidence in approaching God in prayer?

3. Jim shared a story that gives us a glimpse of the hope he has because he serves a God who never changes, who will never back down from his promises. In what ways does the faithful, unchangeable nature of God's character influence your hope and how you pray?

WRAP-UP (9 MINUTES)

Closing DVD Comments from Jim Cymbala

Personal Reflection

Ephesians 6:18 reminds us to "pray in the Spirit on all occasions with all kinds of prayers and requests. With this in mind, be alert and always keep on praying for all the saints." That is what Jim suggested you do at the end of his video presentation. So take time now to think about someone who needs intercessory prayer that the Lord may have brought to your attention during this session.

Perhaps this person has a deep spiritual, physical, or emotional need. Or perhaps you just know, through the Holy Spirit's guidance, that this person needs prayer. Take a few moments right now to pray quietly for the person the Lord has brought to your mind. Ask the Holy Spirit to guide you in intercession and perhaps bring to mind a scriptural promise to include in your prayer.

Group Prayer

Briefly share with your group the person whom the Lord brought to your mind who needs prayer. Be sensitive to personal situations, however. You may need to avoid mentioning a person by name or being too specific about a need that would identify someone inappropriately. Then lift up your hearts together, praying for each person mentioned. Expect to see great changes because you have come together to bring those needs to God who says, "nothing is too hard for me."

> "All of us at times need other believers to strengthen and encourage our faith.... Each of us can at times help other believers by strengthening and encouraging their faith."
> *Breakthrough Prayer,*
> *p. 181*

PERSONAL JOURNEY: TO DO ON YOUR OWN

Interceding for others through prayer is a great privilege and responsibility. Time and time again, the Bible shows us the importance of intercessory prayer. Epaphras, for example, is described as "always wrestling in prayer for you, that you may stand firm in all the will of God, mature and fully assured" (Colossians 4:12).

> "Jesus said, 'Men ought always to pray and not give up,' and the reason he said don't give up is because the answers don't come on our timetable. The answers come when God decrees they will come."
> From the video

Although the work of intercessory prayer is often difficult, it is to be a key part of every believer's life. As is true in all things, Jesus is both our teacher and example. He taught us how to persevere in prayer and often prayed for others.

Bible Discovery

1. What is Jesus doing for all believers—his church—right now, and what should this inspire us to do? (See Romans 8:34.)

2. During his ministry on earth, Jesus often prayed for other people. What do you learn from each of the following prayers of Jesus? What do they mean to you? What do they inspire you to do?

   a. For his murderers: Luke 23:32–34

   b. For his disciples: John 17:6–19

c. For all believers: John 17:20–26

d. For Simon Peter: Luke 22:31–32

My Personal Prayer Journal

God, whom I serve with my whole heart
in preaching the gospel of his Son, is my witness how constantly
I remember you in my prayers at all times.
ROMANS 1:9–10

During the days and weeks ahead, continue to pray for people whom the Holy Spirit lays on your heart. Keep praying for them, no matter how bleak circumstances seem to be. Rely on God's promises in his Word, and remember that he — more than anyone else — desires to respond to your faith and show himself powerful.

Use the following pages to jot down any thoughts, ideas, or questions this session has generated. And continue to journal what God reveals to you through prayer and how he answers your prayers.

My Personal Prayer Journal

Then Jesus told his disciples a parable to show them
that they should always pray and not give up.
LUKE 18:1

Session Six

Creating a Prayer Ministry in Your Church

My house will be called a house of prayer.
MATTHEW 21:13

INTRODUCTION (5 MINUTES)

Our final session together focuses on practical ways by which we, as pastors and lay leaders, can encourage a new or renewed focus on prayer in our churches. If you are a pastor, take careful note of Jim Cymbala's "nuts and bolts" suggestions for guiding your church toward becoming more of a house of prayer. If you are a lay leader, and your pastor(s) has not yet seen this video teaching series, take note of some of the things that you think could make prayer a higher

> "I pray that anyone who watches this will be inspired to seek the Lord in a new way ... and take these truths and apply them in your local situation with the guidance and help of the Holy Spirit."
> Adapted from video

priority in the life and worship of your church. When the time is right, share your hopes and insights with your pastor(s) in ways that foster love and cooperation.

Great things will happen as we pray, seek to make each of our churches a house of prayer, and allow God to pour out fresh grace and blessing on us. The point is not to try to copy what the

91

Brooklyn Tabernacle, or any other church, is doing. What's most important is for us to ask the Lord, "What's the next step for us, and for our church?"

Question to Think About

How important a role does prayer play and what is it currently accomplishing in the life and ministry of your church?

DVD TEACHING SEGMENT (20 MINUTES)

Notes

Hitting all the notes of the chord

Prayer: barometer of spiritual maturity

Making prayer a priority

Taking the right steps for your church

Cultivating an atmosphere of prayer

GROUP DISCUSSION (18 MINUTES)

> "If we do not yearn and pray and expect God to stretch out his hand and do the supernatural, it will not happen. That is the simple truth of the matter. We must give him room to operate. If we go on, week after week, filling the time with religious lectures and nothing more, God has little opportunity in which to move."
>
> *Fresh Wind, Fresh Fire*, p. 145

1. Jim described the ministry of the church in terms of notes of a musical chord.

   a. What did he say results when a church has some of the notes such as praise, worship, and teaching, but neglects prayer? What does prayer do that nothing else can?

   b. What are the strong notes in the ministry of your church?

   c. Which note(s) are missing, and what impact is that having on your church, its people, your community?

"The prayer meeting is really a very excellent barometer of the spiritual maturity of any given church. That's just a matter of fact. You can tell how popular the church is by who comes on Sunday morning and how popular the pastor or guest speaker is by who comes on Sunday night or for a special meeting. But you can really find out how much the people really know God and love Jesus by who will come just to wait on the Lord in prayer."

Adapted from video

2. Using prayer as the barometer of the spiritual maturity of a church, how would you assess — on a scale of one to ten, with ten being the highest — the spiritual maturity of your church? Why did you select this number?

What specific changes in relationship to prayer do you think would improve the spiritual maturity of your church?

What specific things can you do to encourage prayer while being sensitive to other people (including pastors and church leaders)?

> "The feature that is supposed to distinguish Christian churches, Christian people, and Christian gatherings is the aroma of prayer. It doesn't matter what your tradition or my tradition is. The house is not ours anyway; it is the Father's. . . . I have seen God do more in people's lives during ten minutes of real prayer than in ten of my sermons."
>
> *Fresh Wind, Fresh Fire*, p. 71

3. How convinced are your church leaders that prayer must be a main priority in the spiritual life of your church? How convinced are the people who attend your church that prayer must be a main priority?

4. What needs to happen within your church leaders and the people who attend your church in order for everyone to be drawn toward waiting on God and spending time in his presence in prayer?

"The format of a prayer meeting is not nearly as important as its essence — touching the Almighty, crying out with one's whole being. I have been in noisy prayer meetings that were mainly a show. I have been with groups in times of silent prayer that were deeply spiritual. The atmosphere of the meeting may vary; what matters most is that we encounter the God of the universe, not just each other."

Fresh Wind, Fresh Fire, p. 30

5. What do you think an "atmosphere of prayer" looks like in a church? Share several examples that illustrate what you mean.

In what ways does the "atmosphere of prayer" in the lives of individual church leaders and individual people in the congregation affect the atmosphere of your whole church?

In what ways does the "atmosphere of prayer" affect all other ministries in your church?

"You can't copy what another church is doing when it comes to prayer because we're all in a different spiritual condition. . . . What we can't do is model ourselves after someone else because what's more important is, 'Lord, what's the next step for me?'"

Adapted from the video

6. What might be the next steps for your church to take to make prayer more of a priority? Discuss several options. For example: Is it a prayer meeting? Is it more time for corporate prayer within the worship service? Is it a preaching series about prayer? Is it a change in attitude and example of church leaders?

WRAP-UP (12 MINUTES)

Personal Reflection

When Jesus, quoting Isaiah 56:7, said that God wants his house to be called "a house of prayer for all nations" (Mark 11:17), he wasn't laying down a legalistic burden. Rather, he was pointing out the secret to possessing God's promises. We need to realize that the promises that overflow our Bibles will overflow into our own lives only as we appropriate them through prayer.

As this final session concludes, take a few minutes to review what you have learned through this series and consider the following questions:

- How has this series inspired you to seek the Lord in new ways?

- What do you want to see God accomplish in your own life through prayer?

- What do you want to see him accomplish in the life of your church?

- What are you willing to do to help your church discover the blessing of becoming a house of prayer?

Group Prayer

> "Let's not play games with ourselves. . . . When the apostles were unjustly arrested, imprisoned, and threatened, they didn't call for a protest; they didn't reach for some political leverage. Instead, they headed to a prayer meeting. Soon the place was vibrating with the power of the Holy Spirit."
>
> *Fresh Wind, Fresh Fire,* p. 73

The apostles had this instinct: When in trouble, pray. When intimidated, pray. When challenged, pray. When persecuted, pray. Prayer is no less important for the church today. Prayer empowers us to live for Christ and drives the ministry of the church. So as you close this session with the other members of your group, humble yourselves before God in prayer.

- Praise God for his unchanging character.
- Ask God to purge you of sin, to fill you with his Spirit, and to draw you closer to himself.
- Thank God for his commitment to keep his promises and to hear and answer our prayers.
- Ask God to give you wisdom in applying at home and in your church what you have learned through these sessions.

- Call on God to use you in a special way to strengthen the prayer life of the church you attend or in which you minister.
- Ask God to help you persevere when discouraging times come into your life or into the life of your church.
- Close your prayer time with the certainty that God has wonderful things ahead for you, other participants in your group, and your church.

God is looking for people who will totally and passionately seek him, who are determined that every thought and action will be pleasing in his sight. For such a person or group, God will prove himself mighty! His power will explode on their behalf! Will you and your church be such people?

PERSONAL JOURNEY: TO DO ON YOUR OWN

"The early Christians began dynamically in power. They were unified, prayerful, filled with the Holy Spirit, going out to do God's work in God's way, and seeing results that glorified him. The hour seemed golden. This was truly the church overcoming the gates of hell, as Jesus described."

Fresh Wind, Fresh Fire, p. 93

Nothing is too big for God to handle, so keep praying! Bring your needs — and those of your church community — to God. He loves to show himself strong in an environment of need. He wants us to petition him for the very things he has promised! He wants your prayers to empower the life of his church. So keep praying!

Bible Discovery

During the times that will come when you lose perspective and feel that you don't want to pray or that your prayers don't matter, look to Solomon's prayer example in 1 Kings 3:7–9. It's a good reminder of how to pray, our attitude in prayer, and the purpose of our prayers:

1. **Solomon approached God first with thanks and praise:** "Now, O LORD my God, you have made your servant king in place of my father David" (v. 7a). Like Solomon, we should approach God with praise on our lips. God is the source of everything we are and have.

2. **Solomon prayed with great humility:** "But I am only a little child and do not know how to carry out my duties" (v. 7b). If we humble ourselves before God, he will lift us up. But if we rely on our own abilities, connections, or position, we will receive little help from God.

3. **Solomon defined himself as God's servant, ready to do his will:** "Your servant is here among the people you have chosen, a great people, too numerous to count or number" (v. 8). Our prayers are not only about us; they are about how God wants us to serve him.

4. **Solomon asked for a blessing that would bless God's people:** "So give your servant a discerning heart to govern your people and to distinguish between right and wrong" (v. 9). This final portion of Solomon's prayer was the real key to God's overwhelming response. Rather than asking selfishly for himself, Solomon called on the Lord for help so that *he might serve God's people effectively.*

My Personal Prayer Journal

They raised their voices together in prayer to God.... After they prayed, the place where they were meeting was shaken. And they were all filled with the Holy Spirit and spoke the word of God boldly.
ACTS 4:24, 31

Continue to pray, calling on the name of the Lord regularly. Ask God to use you, and other people you know, to strengthen the prayer life of your church. Use the following pages to write down your prayer requests for your church to become more of a house of prayer. Write down ideas you have for strengthening the prayer life of your church and ask God to show you the right time to share these. As time goes on, continue to journal your prayer requests and God's answers. He wants to use you and bless you as you seek him in prayer.

My Personal Prayer Journal

They went upstairs to the room where they were staying.
Those present were Peter, John, James and Andrew;
Philip and Thomas, Bartholomew and Matthew; James son
of Alphaeus and Simon the Zealot, and Judas son of James.
They all joined together constantly in prayer, along with the women
and Mary the mother of Jesus, and with his brothers.

ACTS 1:13–14

Fresh Wind, Fresh Fire

What Happens When God's Spirit Invades the Hearts of His People

Jim Cymbala with Dean Merrill

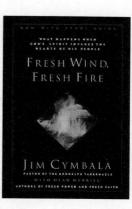

In 1972 the Brooklyn Tabernacle's spark was almost out. Then the Holy Spirit lit a fire that couldn't be quenched.

Pastor Jim Cymbala shares the lessons he learned when the Spirit ignited his heart and began to move through his people. This unforgettable story will set a fire burning in your own heart to experience God's mercy, power, and love as though for the first time.

"This is an important book for all those whose Christianity has become still and sterile. *Fresh Wind, Fresh Fire* signals that God is at work in our day and that he wishes to be at work in our lives."

—DR. JOSEPH M. STOWELL

"This book will drive you to your knees. Be prepared to be provoked but also greatly challenged. You can be sure that reading this book will change you forever."

—DAVID WILKERSON

Softcover 0-310-25153-2

Audio CD, Unabridged 0-310-23649-5
Audio Download, Unabridged 0-310-26152-X

Pick up a copy today at your favorite bookstore!

Fresh Faith

What Happens When Real Faith Ignites God's People

Jim Cymbala with Dean Merrill

Like a Fountain of Clear Water Cleansing a Stagnant, Cynical Culture . . .

FRESH FAITH

Pastor Jim Cymbala calls us back to a fiery, passionate preoccupation with God that will restore what the enemy has stolen from us: our first love for Jesus, our zeal, our troubled children, our wounded marriages, our broken and divided churches.

Born out of the heart and soul of the Brooklyn Tabernacle, the message of *Fresh Faith* is illustrated by true stories of men and women whose lives have been changed through the power of faith.

The same faith that can transform your life—starting today, if you choose.

Softcover 0-310-25155-9

Audio CD, Unabridged 0-310-23639-8
Audio Download, Unabridged 0-310-26149-X

Pick up a copy today at your favorite bookstore!

ZONDERVAN®
.com

Fresh Power

Experiencing the Vast Resources of the Spirit of God

Jim Cymbala with Dean Merrill

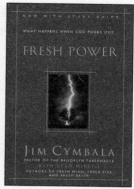

Pastor Jim Cymbala of the Brooklyn Tabernacle has taught his congregation how God's mighty power can infuse their present-day lives and the mission of their church. He continued that teaching nationally in his bestselling books *Fresh Wind, Fresh Fire* and *Fresh Faith*, which tell about the transforming power of God's love to convert prostitutes, addicts, the homeless, and people of all races and stations in life.

Now in *Fresh Power* Cymbala continues to spread the word about the power of God's Holy Spirit in the lives of those who seek him. Fresh power, Cymbala says, is available to us as we desire the Holy Spirit's constant infilling and learn what it means to be Spirit filled, both as individuals and as the church. With the book of Acts as the basis for his study, Cymbala shows how the daily lives of first-century Christians were defined by their belief in God's Word, in the constant infilling of his Spirit, and in the clear and direct responses of obedience to Scripture. He shows that that same life in Christ through the power of the Holy Spirit is available today for pastors, leaders, and laypeople who are longing for revival.

Softcover 0-310-25154-0

Audio Download, Abridged 0-310-26044-2
Audio Download, Unabridged 0-310-26150-3

Pick up a copy today at your favorite bookstore!

ZONDERVAN®
.com

Breakthrough Prayer

The Secret of Receiving What You Need from God

Jim Cymbala

A practical and visionary approach to the principles of prayer that will revolutionize our lives — and enable us to receive all God has for us

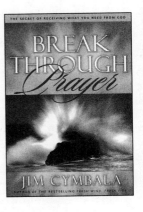

Many people are missing the great things God wants to do in their lives because they don't know how to receive answers to their prayers. This revolutionary book is not a step-by-step guide on how to pray but an inspiring vision that moves people to greater hope as they see the tremendous potential of prayer.

Breakthrough Prayer is peppered with amazing stories of answered prayer from the Brooklyn Tabernacle, including the story of the final survivor of the World Trade Center collapse and the prayers she prayed before becoming the last person pulled from the wreckage alive.

Unique features include:

- *Breakthrough to Holiness:* What is the connection between how we live and how we pray?
- *Breakthrough to Power:* What are the prayers that really have power with God?
- *Breakthrough to Listening:* How can we learn to recognize God's answers to our prayers?

Jesus said and did only the things he received from the Father. When we do the same, the real potential of our lives will unfold, and prayer will enable us to become people with instructed tongues who are able to sustain others in fearful times — times much like those we face today.

Softcover 0-310-25518-X   Audio Download, Unabridged 0-310-26139-2

We want to hear from you. Please send your comments about this book to us in care of zreview@zondervan.com. Thank you.

ZONDERVAN.com/
AUTHORTRACKER
follow your favorite authors